# Easy Home Cooking™

# NO-BAKE
## desserts

**Publications International, Ltd.**
Favorite Brand Name Recipes at www.fbnr.com

**Microwave Cooking:** Microwave ovens vary in wattage. Use the cooking times as guidelines and check for doneness before adding more time.

# CONTENTS

## Not Out of the Oven     6
No-bake desserts are the perfect summertime delights.
No oven? No problem!

## Frozen Desserts and Ice Cream     46
We all scream for these taste-tempting treasures popping out
of your freezer.

## Smoothies and Summer Refreshers     64
Cool off on hot days with a bevy of blissful beverages. A few
ingredients and a big thirst are all you need.

## Berries, Berries, Berries!     70
Strawberries, blueberries, raspberries, blackberries–loads of goodies
featuring summer's bounty. And they're all "berry" delicious.

## Home for the Summer     80
Treat the kids to a fun-filled vacation–without leaving your house.
These sweet snacks are so scrumptious, your kids may never go
back to school!

## Index     93

## Acknowledgments     94

pp. 64 and 68

# Not Out of the Oven

## No-Bake Pineapple Marmalade Squares

▌▌▌

1 cup graham cracker crumbs
½ cup plus 2 tablespoons sugar, divided
¼ cup light margarine, melted
1 cup fat free or light sour cream
4 ounces light cream cheese, softened
¼ cup orange marmalade or apricot fruit spread, divided
1 can (20 ounces) DOLE® Crushed Pineapple, undrained
1 envelope unflavored gelatin

• Combine graham cracker crumbs, 2 tablespoons sugar and margarine in 8-inch square glass baking dish; pat mixture firmly and evenly onto bottom of dish. Freeze 10 minutes.

• Beat sour cream, cream cheese, remaining ½ cup sugar and 1 tablespoon marmalade in medium bowl until smooth and blended; set aside.

• Drain pineapple; reserve ¼ cup juice.

• Sprinkle gelatin over reserved juice in small saucepan; let stand 1 minute. Cook and stir over low heat until gelatin dissolves.

• Beat gelatin mixture into sour cream mixture until well blended. Spoon mixture evenly over crust.

• Stir together pineapple and remaining 3 tablespoons marmalade in small bowl until blended. Evenly spoon over sour cream filling. Cover and refrigerate 2 hours or until firm.
*Makes 16 servings*

# Lemon Raspberry Tiramisu

▌▌▌

2 packages (8 ounces each) fat-free cream cheese, softened
6 packages sugar substitute *or* equivalent of ¼ cup sugar
1 teaspoon vanilla
1 package (0.3 ounce) sugar-free lemon-flavored gelatin
2 cups thawed fat-free nondairy whipped topping
½ cup all-fruit red raspberry preserves
2 tablespoons marsala wine
2 packages (3 ounces each) ladyfingers
1 pint fresh raspberries or frozen unsweetened raspberries, thawed

**1.** Combine cream cheese, sugar substitute and vanilla in large bowl. Beat with electric mixer at high speed until smooth; set aside.

**2.** Combine ⅓ cup water and gelatin in small microwavable bowl; microwave at HIGH 30 seconds to 1 minute or until water is boiling and gelatin is dissolved. Cool slightly.

**3.** Add gelatin mixture to cheese mixture; beat 1 minute. Add whipped topping; beat 1 minute more, scraping side of bowl. Set aside.

**4.** Whisk together preserves, ¼ cup water and marsala in small bowl until well blended. Reserve 2 tablespoons of preserves mixture; set aside. Spread ⅓ cup preserves mixture evenly over bottom of 11×7-inch glass baking dish.

**5.** Split ladyfingers in half; place half in bottom of baking dish. Spread ½ of cheese mixture evenly over ladyfingers; sprinkle 1 cup raspberries evenly over cheese mixture. Top with remaining ladyfingers; spread remaining preserves mixture over ladyfingers. Top with remaining cheese mixture. Cover; refrigerate for at least 2 hours. Sprinkle with remaining raspberries and drizzle with reserved 2 tablespoons preserves mixture before serving.          *Makes 12 servings*

# Chilled Lemon Pie

▋▋▋

**1 envelope unflavored gelatin**
**¼ cup lemon juice**
**2 packages (8 ounces each) PHILADELPHIA® Cream Cheese, softened**
**½ cup sugar**
**1 container (8 ounces) lemon yogurt**
**½ teaspoon grated lemon peel**
**1 cup whipping cream, whipped**
**1 (9-inch) baked pastry shell Currant Raspberry Sauce (recipe follows)**

**SPRINKLE** gelatin over juice in small saucepan. Let stand 5 minutes to soften. Cook and stir on low heat until gelatin is completely dissolved. *Do not boil.*

**MIX** cream cheese and sugar with electric mixer on medium speed until well blended. Blend in yogurt and peel. Stir in gelatin. Refrigerate until mixture is slightly thickened, but not set.

**FOLD** in whipped cream. Spoon into crust. Refrigerate several hours or overnight until firm. Serve with sauce.

*Makes 8 to 10 servings*

*Chilled Lemon Pie*

**CURRANT RASPBERRY SAUCE**
**1 package (10 ounces) frozen
   red raspberries, thawed**
**½ cup KRAFT® Red Currant
   Jelly**
**4 teaspoons cornstarch**

PLACE raspberries and jelly in food processor fitted with steel blade or blender container; cover. Process until well blended. Strain.

STIR cornstarch and raspberry mixture in small saucepan until smooth. Bring to boil on medium heat, stirring constantly. Cook until thickened, stirring constantly. Cool. Serve with pie.

# Chocolate Rice Pudding

█ █ █

**2 cups water**
**1 cup uncooked
   UNCLE BEN'S®
   Converted® Brand Rice**
**2 tablespoons butter**
**¼ cup sugar**
**2 teaspoons cornstarch**
**2 cups milk**
**½ teaspoon vanilla**
**2 egg yolks**
**½ cup semisweet chocolate
   chips**

**1.** Bring water to a boil in large saucepan. Stir in rice and butter. Reduce heat; cover and simmer 20 minutes. Remove from heat. Let stand covered until all liquid is absorbed, about 5 minutes.

**2.** Combine sugar and cornstarch in small bowl; add to hot rice in saucepan. Stir in milk.

**3.** Bring mixture to a boil, stirring occasionally. Boil 1 minute, stirring constantly. Remove from heat; stir in vanilla.

**4.** Beat egg yolks in small bowl. Stir about 1 cup of hot rice mixture into beaten egg yolks.

**5.** Stir egg yolk mixture back into remaining rice mixture in saucepan.

**6.** Cook rice mixture over medium heat, stirring frequently, just until mixture starts to bubble. Remove from heat; add chocolate chips and stir until melted.

**7.** Spoon into individual serving dishes. Chill.
*Makes 6 servings*

# Raspberry-Lemon Gelatin Salad

▌▌▌

1 (10-ounce) package frozen
     raspberries, thawed
   Cold water
1 (3-ounce) package
     raspberry flavored gelatin
1 envelope unflavored gelatin
½ cup lemon juice
2 cups cold milk
1 (3½-ounce) package lemon
     instant pudding and pie
     filling mix
1 cup MIRACLE WHIP® Salad
     Dressing

Drain raspberries, reserving liquid. Add enough water to reserved liquid to measure ¾ cup; set aside. Bring 1 cup water to boil. Gradually add to raspberry flavored gelatin, stirring until dissolved. Stir in reserved raspberry liquid. Cover; chill until thickened but not set. Fold in raspberries. Pour into 1½-quart clear serving bowl. Cover; chill until almost set. Combine unflavored gelatin and lemon juice in small saucepan; let stand 1 minute. Stir over low heat until gelatin is dissolved. Cool. Combine milk and pudding mix; mix as directed on package for pudding. Stir in salad dressing. Gradually add gelatin mixture, mixing until well blended. Pour over raspberry layer; cover. Chill until firm.

*Makes 8 to 10 servings*

# No-Bake Banana Peanut Butter Fudge Bars

▌▌▌

1 ripe, large DOLE® Banana
⅔ cup butter or margarine
2 teaspoons vanilla extract
2½ cups rolled oats
½ cup packed brown sugar
1 cup semisweet chocolate
     chips
½ cup peanut butter

• Finely chop banana (1¼ cups). Melt butter in large skillet over medium heat; stir in vanilla. Add oats and brown sugar. Heat and stir 5 minutes. Set aside ¾ cup oat mixture. Press remaining oat mixture into greased 9-inch square baking pan. Sprinkle banana over crust.

• Melt chocolate and peanut butter together over low heat. Pour and spread over banana. Sprinkle with reserved oat mixture; press down lightly. Chill 2 hours before cutting. Store in refrigerator.

*Makes 24 bars*

# Smucker's® English Berry Pudding

▎▎▎

**12 to 16 slices white bread, crusts removed, cut into half or quarter triangles**
**1 cup SMUCKER'S® Raspberry Preserves**
**2 cups *each* raspberries, blueberries and sliced strawberries (fresh or frozen)**

Line deep 1½- to 2-quart bowl with plastic wrap. Line bottom and side of bowl with half of triangle bread slices. Completely cover surface so no gaps remain between bread slices.

Heat preserves and 6 cups mixed berries in saucepan over high heat. Bring to a boil and simmer 5 minutes to release juices. Spoon half of berry mixture into bread-lined bowl. Cover with half of remaining bread triangles and remaining berry mixture. Cover second layer of berries with remaining bread. Use more bread if needed to completely seal bowl. Cover pudding with plastic wrap.

Place plate over bowl to weigh it down. Refrigerate pudding 12 to 24 hours before serving.

To serve, remove plate and plastic wrap. Unmold bowl onto serving plate. Remove bowl and carefully peel plastic wrap from pudding. Serve pudding dusted with powdered sugar, whipped cream, frozen yogurt or whipped topping.

*Makes 8 servings*

# Rocky Road Cheesecake Squares

▎▎▎

**1 (11¾-ounce) package ROYAL® Chocolate Cheesecake**
**⅓ cup margarine, melted**
**3 tablespoons sugar**
**1½ cups cold milk**
**½ cup mini-marshmallows**
**⅓ cup PLANTERS® Walnuts, chopped**
**⅓ cup semisweet chocolate chips**
**Whipped topping, for garnish**

In small bowl, combine graham cracker crumbs, margarine and sugar. Press mixture on bottom of 8×8×2-inch pan. Chill. Meanwhile, prepare cheesecake filling according to package directions using milk; fold in marshmallows, walnuts and chocolate chips. Spread over prepared crust. Chill for 1 hour. To serve, cut into squares; garnish with whipped topping.

*Makes 9 servings*

# Funky Devil's Fudge Sauce

▊▊▊

1 can (14 ounces) sweetened condensed milk (not evaporated milk)
1 package (12 ounces) semi-sweet chocolate chips
¼ cup whole milk
3 tablespoons FRANK'S® REDHOT® Hot Sauce
Ice cream or pound cake (optional)

Combine condensed milk, chocolate and whole milk in large microwavable bowl. Microwave at HIGH 3 minutes or until chocolate is melted, stirring once. Add REDHOT® sauce; stir until smooth. Serve over ice cream or cake. Garnish as desired. Refrigerate any leftover sauce.*

*Makes 2½ cups*

*\*Leftover sauce may be reheated in microwave. Microwave and stir for 30 seconds at a time. If sauce becomes too thick, just stir in small amount of whole milk.*

**Note:** This sauce is also great as a fondue dipping sauce. Serve with cubed pound cake, fresh strawberries, oranges segments, apple wedges, sliced peeled kiwifruit and cubed fresh pineapple.

**Prep Time:** 5 minutes
**Cook Time:** 3 minutes

# Cannoli Loaf

▊▊▊

1 (15-ounce) container part-skim ricotta cheese
¼ cup sugar
3 tablespoons fat-free (skim) milk
¼ cup miniature semi-sweet chocolate chips
¼ cup chopped candied cherries
20 HONEY MAID® Grahams
1 cup prepared whipped topping

With mixer, beat cheese, sugar and milk until smooth. Stir in chocolate chips and cherries.

Place 11 crackers on bottom and around sides of plastic wrap-lined 8½×4½×2½-inch loaf pan. Spread ⅓ of cheese mixture over bottom of prepared pan; top with 3 crackers. Repeat 2 more times, ending with crackers. Cover; chill at least 4 hours.

Unmold loaf onto serving plate; remove plastic wrap. Frost with whipped topping; garnish as desired.          *Makes 8 servings*

# Mimosa Mold

▊▊▊

1½ cups boiling water
 1 package (8-serving size) *or*
    2 packages (4-serving
    size) JELL-O® Brand
    Sparkling White Grape or
    Lemon Flavor Gelatin
    Dessert
 2 cups cold seltzer or club
    soda
 1 can (11 ounces) mandarin
    orange segments, drained
 1 cup sliced strawberries

STIR boiling water into gelatin in large bowl at least 2 minutes or until completely dissolved. Refrigerate 15 minutes. Gently stir in seltzer. Refrigerate about 30 minutes or until slightly thickened (consistency of unbeaten egg whites.) Gently stir about 15 seconds. Stir in oranges and strawberries. Pour into 6-cup mold.

REFRIGERATE 4 hours or until firm. Unmold.* Garnish as desired. Store leftover gelatin mold in refrigerator.

*Makes 12 servings*

***Unmolding:** Dip mold in warm water for about 15 seconds. Gently pull gelatin from around edges with moist fingers. Place moistened serving plate on top of mold. Invert mold and plate; holding mold and plate together, shake slightly to loosen. Gently remove mold and center gelatin on plate.*

**Preparation Time:** 15 minutes
**Refrigerating Time:** 4¾ hours

# Tropical Fruit Tart

▊▊▊

1¼ cups BAKER'S® ANGEL
    FLAKE® Coconut, divided
 1 can (15¼ ounces) tropical
    fruit salad, drained,
    reserving juice
 1 tub (8 ounces) COOL WHIP®
    Whipped Topping, thawed
 1 (9-inch) sponge cake layer

TOAST coconut according to package directions.

STIR 1 cup of coconut and ⅓ cup of reserved juice into whipped topping with wire whisk in medium bowl until blended. Brush remaining juice over top of cake layer.

SPREAD whipped topping mixture over cake layer. Top with fruit; sprinkle with remaining ¼ cup coconut.

REFRIGERATE until ready to serve.          *Makes 12 servings*

# Key Lime Pie

■■■

1 cup graham cracker crumbs
3 tablespoons melted
    margarine
1 teaspoon EQUAL® FOR
    RECIPES *or* 3 packets
    EQUAL® sweetener *or*
    2 tablespoons EQUAL®
    SPOONFUL™
1 envelope (¼ ounce)
    unflavored gelatin
1¾ cups skim milk, divided
1 package (8 ounces)
    reduced-fat cream
    cheese, softened
⅓ to ½ cup fresh lime juice
3½ teaspoons EQUAL® FOR
    RECIPES *or* 12 packets
    EQUAL® sweetener *or*
    ½ cup EQUAL®
    SPOONFUL™
Lime slices, raspberries and
    fresh mint sprigs, for
    garnish (optional)

• Combine graham cracker crumbs, margarine and 1 teaspoon Equal® For Recipes *or* 3 packets Equal® sweetener *or* 2 tablespoons Equal® Spoonful™ in bottom of 7-inch springform pan; pat evenly on bottom and ½ inch up side of pan.

• Sprinkle gelatin over ½ cup milk in small saucepan; let stand 2 to 3 minutes. Cook over low heat, stirring constantly, until gelatin is dissolved. Beat cream cheese in small bowl until fluffy; beat in remaining 1¼ cups milk and gelatin mixture. Mix in lime juice and 3½ teaspoons Equal® For Recipes *or* 12 packets Equal® sweetener *or* ½ cup Equal® Spoonful™. Refrigerate pie until set, about 2 hours.

• To serve, loosen side of pie from pan with small spatula and remove side of pan. Place pie on serving plate; garnish with lime slices, raspberries and mint, if desired.

*Makes 8 servings*

# Fresh Strawberry Lime Pudding

▌▌▌

1½ cups sugar
3 tablespoons cornstarch
3 tablespoons all-purpose flour
  Dash salt
1½ cups hot water
3 egg yolks, slightly beaten
2 tablespoons butter or
  margarine
½ teaspoon grated lime peel
½ cup lime juice
1 drop green food coloring
  (optional)
6 large strawberries, sliced

Combine sugar, cornstarch, flour and salt in medium saucepan. Gradually add hot water, stirring constantly. Cook and stir over medium-high heat until mixture comes to a boil. Reduce heat to low; cook and stir 2 minutes more. Remove from heat. Stir about ⅓ cup hot sugar mixture into egg yolks; return mixture to saucepan. Bring to a boil and cook 2 minutes, stirring constantly. Stir in butter and lime peel. Slowly add lime juice and food coloring, if desired; mix well. Pour into 6 dessert dishes and refrigerate until chilled. Top with sliced strawberries before serving. *Makes 6 servings*

*Favorite recipe from* **Bob Evans**®

# Englishman's Trifle

▌▌▌

1 box (10 ounces) BIRDS EYE®
  frozen Strawberries*
1 package (3.4 ounces)
  vanilla instant pudding
1½ cups milk
1 cup thawed frozen whipped
  topping
8 thin slices fresh or thawed
  frozen pound cake
½ cup toasted sliced almonds
¼ cup mini semisweet
  chocolate chips (optional)

*Or, substitute Birds Eye® frozen Raspberries.*

• Thaw strawberries according to package directions.

• Prepare pudding with 1½ cups milk according to package directions. Let stand 5 minutes; gently stir in whipped topping.

• Place 1 slice cake in each of 4 individual serving bowls. Spoon half of strawberries over cake. Top with half of pudding mixture, almonds and chocolate chips.

• Repeat layers of cake, strawberries, pudding, almonds and chips. Cover and chill until ready to serve.
*Makes 4 servings*

# Blackberry Lemon Cheesecake Trifle

▐ ▐ ▐

1 package (8 ounces)
    reduced-fat cream
    cheese, softened
⅓ cup lemon juice
1 can (14 ounces) low-fat
    sweetened condensed
    milk
2 cups frozen whipped
    topping, thawed
1 package (10¾ ounces)
    low-fat frozen pound
    cake, thawed
¼ cup frozen lemonade
    concentrate
1 jar (10 ounces) seedless
    blackberry jam, melted
6 cups fresh or thawed frozen
    blackberries

**1.** Combine cream cheese and lemon juice in small bowl. Beat with electric mixer until smooth. Stir in milk. Fold in whipped topping. Set aside.

**2.** Cut pound cake into ¼-inch-thick slices. Arrange half of cake slices in bottom of large glass bowl or trifle dish.

**3.** Combine lemonade concentrate and ¼ cup water in small bowl. Brush half of lemonade mixture over pound cake; let stand 5 minutes. Brush half of jam over pound cake. Spoon half of cream cheese mixture over jam. Arrange half of berries over top. Repeat layers with remaining ingredients. Cover with plastic wrap; refrigerate overnight.

*Makes 10 to 12 servings*

# Creamy Tapioca Pudding

▐ ▐ ▐

2 cups skim milk
3 tablespoons quick-cooking
    tapioca
1 egg
⅛ teaspoon salt
3½ teaspoons EQUAL® FOR
    RECIPES *or* 12 packets
    EQUAL® sweetener *or*
    ½ cup EQUAL®
    SPOONFUL™
1 to 2 teaspoons vanilla
    Ground cinnamon and
    nutmeg

• Combine milk, tapioca, egg and salt in medium saucepan. Let stand 5 minutes. Cook over medium-high heat, stirring constantly, until boiling. Remove from heat; stir in Equal® and vanilla.

• Spoon mixture into serving dishes; sprinkle lightly with cinnamon and nutmeg. Serve warm, or refrigerate and serve chilled.

*Makes 4 (⅔-cup) servings*

# Mango-Orange Mousse

▌▌▌

**1 large can (28 ounces) mangoes or 2 small cans (15 ounces each) mangoes, drained**
**1 envelope (1 tablespoon) unflavored gelatin**
**¼ cup cold water**
**3 eggs (room temperature), separated**
**¾ cup orange juice**
**½ cup sugar, divided**
**1 tablespoon lemon juice**
**Dash salt**
**2 tablespoons rum**
**1 cup heavy cream, divided**
**Shredded orange peel for garnish**
**Mint sprig for garnish**

Process enough mangoes in blender or food processor container fitted with metal blade to make 1 cup purée. Thinly slice remaining mangoes; cover. Refrigerate; reserve for garnish.

Sprinkle gelatin over cold water in small bowl; let stand 1 minute to soften. Beat egg yolks in heavy 1-quart pan. Whisk in orange juice, ¼ cup sugar, lemon juice and salt. Cook over medium-low heat, stirring constantly, until mixture has thickened enough to lightly coat metal spoon. Remove from heat; add softened gelatin and stir until dissolved. Stir in mango purée and rum. Refrigerate (or stir over ice water) until mixture mounds slightly when dropped from spoon.

Beat egg whites in large bowl of electric mixer on high speed until frothy. Gradually add remaining ¼ cup sugar, 1 tablespoon at a time, beating well after each addition. Beat until stiff peaks form; fold into mango mixture. Without washing bowl or beaters, whip ½ cup cream until soft peaks form. Fold into mango mixture. Spoon into glass serving bowl. Refrigerate until firm, 3 to 4 hours or up to 24 hours. Just before serving, whip remaining ½ cup cream until soft peaks form. Garnish mousse with reserved mango slices, whipped cream, orange peel and mint.

*Makes 6 to 8 servings*

*Mango-Orange Mousse*

# Chocolate Truffle Loaf with Sweet Raspberry Sauce

▌▌▌

**2 cups heavy cream, divided**
**3 egg yolks**
**16 squares (1 ounce each)**
 **semisweet chocolate**
**½ cup KARO® Light or Dark**
 **Corn Syrup**
**½ cup MAZOLA® Margarine**
**¼ cup confectioners' sugar**
**1 teaspoon vanilla**
 **Sweet Raspberry Sauce**
 **(recipe follows)**

**1.** Line 9¼×5¼×2¾-inch loaf pan with plastic wrap.

**2.** In small bowl mix ½ cup cream with egg yolks. In large saucepan combine chocolate, corn syrup and margarine; stir over medium heat until melted. Add egg mixture. Cook 3 minutes over medium heat, stirring constantly. Cool to room temperature.

**3.** In small bowl with mixer at medium speed, beat remaining 1½ cups cream, sugar and vanilla until soft peaks form. Gently fold into chocolate mixture just until combined. Pour into prepared pan; cover with plastic wrap.

**4.** Refrigerate overnight or chill in freezer 3 hours. Slice and serve with Sweet Raspberry Sauce. *Makes 12 servings*

**SWEET RASPBERRY SAUCE:** In blender or food processor purée 1 package (10 ounces) thawed frozen raspberries; strain to remove seeds. Stir in ⅓ cup KARO® Light Corn Syrup.

**MICROWAVE DIRECTIONS:** Prepare pan and egg mixture as directed. In 3-quart microwavable bowl mix chocolate, corn syrup and margarine. Microwave on HIGH 2 to 2½ minutes or until melted, stirring twice. Stir in egg mixture. Microwave 3 minutes, stirring twice. Continue as directed in steps 3 and 4.

**Prep Time:** 30 minutes, plus chilling

*Chocolate Truffle Loaf with Sweet Raspberry Sauce*

# Better-Than-S_x Cake

### ▌▌▌

1½ cups graham cracker
 crumbs
⅔ cup chopped pecans,
 divided
½ cup (1 stick) butter or
 margarine, melted
6 tablespoons sugar
1 package (8 ounces)
 PHILADELPHIA® Cream
 Cheese, softened
3½ cups cold milk
2 packages (4-serving size)
 JELL-O® Vanilla Flavor
 Instant Pudding & Pie
 Filling
1⅓ cups BAKER'S® ANGEL
 FLAKE® Coconut, divided
1 tub (8 ounces) COOL WHIP®
 Whipped Topping, thawed

MIX crumbs, ⅓ cup pecans, butter and sugar in 13×9-inch pan. Press firmly onto bottom of pan.

BEAT cream cheese in large bowl with electric mixer on low speed until smooth. Gradually beat in ½ cup milk. Add remaining milk and pudding mix. Beat on low speed about 2 minutes or until well blended. Stir in 1 cup coconut. Pour immediately over crust. Spread whipped topping evenly over pudding mixture.

REFRIGERATE 2 hours or until set. Toast remaining ⅓ cup coconut and ⅓ cup pecans. Sprinkle over top of dessert.
*Makes 15 servings*

**Preparation Time:** 30 minutes
**Refrigerating Time:** 2 hours

# Rice Pudding Mexicana

### ▌▌▌

1 package instant rice
 pudding
1 tablespoon vanilla
¼ teaspoon ground cinnamon
 Dash ground cloves
¼ cup slivered almonds
 Additional ground cinnamon

**1.** Prepare rice pudding according to package directions.

**2.** Remove pudding from heat; stir in vanilla, ¼ teaspoon cinnamon and cloves. Pour into individual dessert dishes.

**3.** Sprinkle with almonds and additional cinnamon. Serve warm. *Makes 6 servings*

**Prep and Cook Time:** 18 minutes

# White Chocolate Cheesecake

**■ ■ ■**

1 package (11.1 ounces) JELL-O® No Bake Real Cheesecake
⅓ cup butter or margarine, melted
2 tablespoons sugar
1½ cups cold milk
1 package (6 squares) BAKER'S® Premium White Baking Chocolate Squares, melted
2 squares BAKER'S® Semi-Sweet Baking Chocolate, melted (optional)

MIX crumbs, butter and sugar thoroughly with fork in 9-inch pie plate until crumbs are well moistened. Press firmly against side of pie plate first, using finger or large spoon to shape edge. Press remaining crumbs firmly onto bottom of pie plate using measuring cup.

BEAT milk and filling mix with electric mixer on low speed until blended. Beat on medium speed 3 minutes. (Filling will be thick.) Reserve about 3 tablespoons melted white chocolate for garnish, if desired. Stir remaining melted white chocolate into filling mixture. Spoon into crust. Drizzle with reserved melted white chocolate and melted semi-sweet chocolate, if desired.

REFRIGERATE at least 1 hour, if desired. *Makes 8 servings*

**Preparation Time:** 15 minutes
**Refrigerating Time:** 1 hour

*White Chocolate Cheesecake*

# No-Bake Old-Fashioned Coconut Cream Pie

▌▌▌

**2 envelopes KNOX®
Unflavored Gelatine
¼ cup cold water
1 can (15 ounces) cream of
coconut
1 cup light cream or
half-and-half
¾ cup EGG BEATERS® Healthy
Real Egg Substitute
Extra serving size
(9 ounces) prepared
graham cracker crust or
9-inch baked pastry shell**

In small saucepan, sprinkle gelatine over cold water; let stand 1 minute. Stir over low heat until gelatine is completely dissolved, about 3 minutes.

In blender or food processor, process cream of coconut, light cream and Egg Beaters® until blended. While processing, through feed cap, gradually add gelatine mixture and process until blended. Turn into graham cracker crust; chill until firm, about 3 hours. Garnish, if desired, with additional whipped cream and toasted coconut.

*Makes about 12 servings*

# No-Bake Butterscotch Haystacks

▌▌▌

**1 cup HERSHEY'S
Butterscotch Chips
½ cup REESE'S® Peanut
Butter Chips
1 tablespoon shortening (do
not use butter, margarine
or oil)
1½ cups (3-ounce can) chow
mein noodles, coarsely
broken**

**1.** Line cookie sheet with wax paper. Place butterscotch chips, peanut butter chips and shortening in medium microwave-safe bowl.

**2.** Microwave at HIGH (100%) 1 minute; stir. If necessary, microwave at HIGH an additional 15 seconds at a time, stirring after each heating, just until chips are melted and mixture is smooth when stirred.

**3.** Immediately add chow mein noodles; stir to coat. Drop mixture by heaping teaspoons onto prepared cookie sheet or into paper candy cups; let stand until firm. If necessary, cover and refrigerate until firm. Store in refrigerator in tightly covered container.

*Makes about 2 dozen cookies*

**Chocolate Haystacks:**
Substitute 1 cup HERSHEY'S Semi-Sweet Chocolate Chips or HERSHEY'S Milk Chocolate Chips for butterscotch chips. Proceed as directed with peanut butter chips, shortening and chow mein noodles.

# Tiramisu

▌▌▌

2 packages (3 ounces each) ladyfingers, thawed if frozen, split in half horizontally
¾ cup brewed espresso*
2 tablespoons coffee liqueur or brandy (optional)
1 package (8 ounces) cream cheese, softened
2 tablespoons sugar
⅓ cup sour cream
½ cup whipping cream
2 tablespoons unsweetened cocoa powder, divided
Chocolate curls and mint leaves (optional)

*Use fresh brewed espresso, instant espresso powder prepared according to directions on jar or 2 teaspoons instant coffee powder dissolved in ¾ cup hot water.*

Place ladyfingers on baking sheet, uncovered, 8 hours or overnight to dry. Or, dry ladyfingers by placing on microwavable plate. Microwave at MEDIUM-HIGH (70% power) 1 minute; turn ladyfingers over. Microwave at MEDIUM-HIGH 1 to 1½ minutes or until dry.

Combine espresso and liqueur, if desired, in small bowl. Dip half of ladyfingers in espresso mixture; place on bottom of 2-quart serving bowl.

Beat cream cheese and sugar with electric mixer at medium speed until fluffy; add sour cream, beating until blended. Add whipping cream, beating until smooth. Spread half of cheese mixture over ladyfingers.

Place 1 tablespoon cocoa in fine strainer. Lightly tap rim of strainer and dust cocoa over cheese layer.

Dip remaining ladyfingers in espresso mixture. Place over cheese mixture in serving bowl.

Spread remaining cheese mixture over ladyfingers. Dust remaining 1 tablespoon cocoa over cheese layer. Refrigerate, covered, 4 hours or overnight. Garnish with chocolate curls and mint leaves, if desired.
*Makes 6 servings*

# Peanut Butter Chocolate No-Bake Bars

▌▌▌

**BARS**
 1 cup peanut butter
 ½ cup light corn syrup
 ½ cup powdered sugar
 2 tablespoons margarine or
   butter
 2 cups QUAKER® Oats (quick
   or old fashioned,
   uncooked)

**TOPPING**
 1 cup (6 ounces) semisweet
   chocolate pieces
 2 tablespoons peanut butter
 ¼ cup chopped peanuts
   (optional)

**1.** For bars, in medium saucepan, heat 1 cup peanut butter, corn syrup, powdered sugar and margarine over medium-low heat until margarine is melted, stirring frequently. Remove from heat.

**2.** Stir in oats, mixing well.

**3.** Spread onto bottom of *ungreased* 8- or 9-inch square pan; set aside.

**4.** For topping, place chocolate pieces in medium-size microwavable bowl. Microwave on HIGH 1 to 2 minutes, stirring every 30 seconds until smooth.

**5.** Stir in 2 tablespoons peanut butter until well blended. Spread evenly over oats layer. Sprinkle with chopped nuts, if desired.

**6.** Refrigerate 30 minutes or until chocolate is set.

**7.** Cut into bars with sharp knife (4 rows×6 rows). If bars are difficult to cut, let stand about 10 minutes.

*Makes 24 bars*

# No-Bake Cherry Crisps

▌▌▌

 1 cup powdered sugar
 1 cup peanut butter
 ¼ cup butter, softened
 1⅓ cups crisp rice cereal
 ½ cup maraschino cherries,
   drained, dried and chopped
 ¼ cup plus 2 tablespoons mini
   semisweet chocolate
   chips
 ¼ cup chopped pecans
 1 to 2 cups flaked coconut

In large bowl, beat sugar, peanut butter and butter. Stir in cereal, cherries, chocolate chips and pecans. Mix well. Shape teaspoonfuls of dough into 1-inch balls. Roll in coconut. Place on cookie sheets and chill in refrigerator 1 hour. Store in refrigerator.

*Makes about 3 dozen cookies*

# Strawberries and Cream Mousse Cake

1 prepared angel food cake
    (14 to 16 ounces)
¼ cup strawberry jelly
2 cups whipping cream,
    divided
1 pint strawberries, washed
    and hulled, divided
3 tablespoons powdered
    sugar
1 teaspoon vanilla

1. Slice 1 inch layer from top of cake; lift off in 1 piece and set aside. Hollow out cake leaving ¾-inch border on sides and 1-inch border on bottom. Save cake crumbs for another use.

2. Beat jelly in small deep bowl at medium speed of electric mixer. Add 1 cup whipping cream; beat at high speed 2 minutes or until soft peaks form.

3. Chop enough strawberries to measure 1½ cups; fold into whipped cream mixture. Spoon cream mixture into hollowed out cake until even with top of cake. Replace cake top.

4. Whip remaining 1 cup cream in small deep bowl at high speed 2 minutes or until thickened; beat in sugar and vanilla until soft peaks form. Frost cake with whipped cream.

5. Cut remaining strawberries in half. Arrange on cake.

*Makes 10 servings*

*Strawberries and Cream Mousse Cake*

# Banana Pistachio Pie

▌▌▌

¾ cup cinnamon graham
    cracker crumbs
2 tablespoons reduced-fat
    margarine, melted
2 packages (4-serving size
    each) fat-free sugar-free
    pistachio instant pudding
    and pie mix
2½ cups fat-free (skim) milk
1 large ripe banana, sliced
¼ teaspoon ground cinnamon
1 cup thawed frozen reduced-
    fat nondairy whipped
    topping
    Additional thawed frozen
    reduced-fat nondairy
    whipped topping
    (optional)

**1.** Combine graham cracker crumbs and margarine in small bowl, stirring with fork until crumbly. Press onto bottom of 9-inch pie plate.

**2.** Prepare pudding mix according to manufacturer's pie directions, using 2½ cups milk. Gently stir in banana and cinnamon; fold in 1 cup whipped topping. Pour into prepared crust. Refrigerate at least 1 hour. Top with additional whipped cream before serving, if desired.

*Makes 8 servings*

# Southern Ambrosia

▌▌▌

3 cups fresh pineapple
    chunks
2 bananas, sliced
3 cans (15 ounces each)
    mandarin orange
    segments, drained
1 jar (6 ounces) maraschino
    cherries, drained
½ cup coarsely chopped
    pecans, toasted
1¼ cups BAKER'S® ANGEL
    FLAKE® Coconut
1 tub (8 ounces) COOL WHIP®
    Whipped Topping, thawed

**LAYER** half of pineapple, bananas, oranges, cherries and pecans in straight-sided glass bowl. Sprinkle with half of coconut. Repeat layers.

**TOP** with whipped topping, spreading to edge of bowl to seal. Decorate with additional maraschino cherries, pecan halves and toasted coconut.

**REFRIGERATE** until ready to serve. *Makes 6 cups*

**Prep Time:** 15 minutes

*Banana Pistachio Pie*

# Peach Melba Dessert

▌▌▌

**1½ cups boiling water, divided**
**2 packages (4-serving size) JELL-O® Brand Raspberry Flavor Sugar Free Low Calorie Gelatin Dessert or JELL-O® Brand Raspberry Flavor Gelatin Dessert, divided**
**1 container (8 ounces) BREYERS® Vanilla Lowfat Yogurt**
**1 cup raspberries, divided**
**1 can (8 ounces) peach slices in juice, undrained**
**Cold water**

**STIR** ¾ cup boiling water into 1 package of gelatin in large bowl at least 2 minutes or until completely dissolved. Refrigerate about 1 hour or until slightly thickened (consistency of unbeaten egg whites). Stir in yogurt and ½ cup raspberries. Reserve remaining raspberries for garnish. Pour gelatin mixture into serving bowl. Refrigerate about 2 hours or until set but not firm (gelatin should stick to finger when touched and should mound).

**MEANWHILE,** drain peaches, reserving juice. Add cold water to reserved juice to make 1 cup; set aside. Stir remaining ¾ cup boiling water into remaining package gelatin in large bowl at least 2 minutes or until completely dissolved. Stir in measured juice and water. Refrigerate about 1 hour or until slightly thickened (consistency of unbeaten egg whites).

**RESERVE** several peach slices for garnish; chop remaining peaches. Stir chopped peaches into slightly thickened gelatin. Spoon over gelatin layer in bowl. Refrigerate 3 hours or until firm. Top with reserved peach slices and raspberries.
*Makes 8 servings*

**Preparation Time:** 20 minutes
**Refrigerating Time:** 6 hours

# Chocolate Dessert Timbales

███

1 envelope unflavored gelatin
½ cup cold water
⅓ cup sugar
3 tablespoons HERSHEY'S Cocoa
1½ cups low-fat (1%) milk
2 egg yolks, slightly beaten
2 teaspoons vanilla extract
1 cup frozen light nondairy whipped topping, thawed
Additional whipped topping
Fresh raspberries or canned fruit slices, drained

Sprinkle gelatin over cold water in small bowl; let stand several minutes to soften.

Stir together sugar and cocoa in medium saucepan; gradually stir in milk. Stir in egg yolks. Cook over medium heat, stirring constantly, until mixture just begins to boil; remove from heat. Stir in reserved gelatin mixture and vanilla; stir until gelatin is completely dissolved. Transfer to medium bowl; refrigerate, stirring occasionally, until mixture begins to set.

Carefully fold 1 cup whipped topping into chocolate mixture, blending until smooth. Pour into 6 small serving dishes or custard cups; refrigerate until set. Garnish with additional whipped topping and fruit.

*Makes 6 servings*

# Lemon Blueberry Layer Cake

███

1 (10.75-ounce) pound cake, sliced into 10 slices
2 (10-ounce) jars KNOTT'S® Blueberry Preserves
2 (4-cup packs) HUNT'S® Snack Pack Lemon Pudding
Grated peel from 1 lemon
1 (8-ounce) tub frozen whipped topping, thawed

Arrange cake slices on bottom of 13×9×2-inch pan. Reserve and set aside *3 tablespoons* preserves. Spread *remaining* preserves over cake slices. In small bowl, combine pudding with lemon peel (for a tarter lemon flavor, add 2 tablespoons lemon juice to filling); mix well. Spread filling over preserves then top with whipped topping. Cover and refrigerate until ready to serve. Just before serving, randomly swirl in *remaining* preserves.

*Makes 10 servings*

*Chocolate Dessert Timbales*

# Fluffy Cheesecake

▌▌▌

**1 package (8 ounces) PHILADELPHIA® Cream Cheese, softened**
**⅓ cup sugar**
**1 tub (8 ounces) COOL WHIP® Whipped Topping, thawed**
**1 prepared graham cracker crumb crust (6 ounces *or* 9 inches)**

**BEAT** cream cheese and sugar in large bowl with wire whisk or electric mixer on high speed until smooth. Gently stir in whipped topping. Spoon into crust.

**REFRIGERATE** 3 hours or until set. Garnish as desired.

*Makes 8 servings*

**Fluffy Cherry Cheesecake:** Prepare and refrigerate as directed. Spoon 1½ cups cherry pie filling over top of pie.

**Fluffy Cranberry Cheesecake:** Beat in 1 cup whole berry cranberry sauce with cream cheese. Proceed as directed.

**Fluffy Pumpkin Cheesecake:** Increase sugar to ½ cup. Beat in 1 cup canned pumpkin and ½ teaspoon pumpkin pie spice with cream cheese. Proceed as directed.

**Fluffy Caramel Pecan Cheesecake:** Beat cream cheese and sugar in large bowl with wire whisk until smooth. Gently stir in whipped topping. Spoon 1 cup cream cheese mixture into crust; spread evenly. Top with ⅓ cup KRAFT® Caramel Topping and ¼ cup toasted pecans; spread evenly. Top with remaining cream cheese mixture. Refrigerate 3 hours or until set. Garnish with additional caramel topping, whipped topping and pecans.

**Prep Time:** 15 minutes

## Hot Bananas with Rum and Chocolate

■ ■ ■

2 tablespoons butter
2 tablespoons dark brown
    sugar
2 tablespoons honey
¾ teaspoon TABASCO® brand
    Pepper Sauce
4 ripe bananas, peeled and
    sliced into 1-inch rounds
3 tablespoons dark rum
4 (¼-cup) scoops vanilla ice
    cream
    Chocolate flavored syrup

Combine butter, brown sugar, honey and TABASCO® Sauce in large skillet; cook over medium-high heat until mixture sizzles. Add bananas and toss gently, until coated.

Turn heat to high, add rum and cook 20 seconds or until mixture has syrupy consistency and bananas are glazed.

Scoop ice cream into bowls and spoon warm bananas on top. Drizzle with chocolate sauce and serve immediately.

*Makes 4 servings*

## Angel Food Cake with Pineapple Sauce

■ ■ ■

1 can (20 ounces) DOLE®
    Crushed Pineapple,
    undrained
2 tablespoons sugar
1 tablespoon cornstarch
1 tablespoon orange
    marmalade, peach or
    apricot fruit spread
1 prepared angel food cake

• Combine pineapple with juice, sugar, cornstarch and orange marmalade in small saucepan. Bring to a boil. Reduce heat to low; cook, stirring constantly, 2 minutes or until sauce thickens. Cool slightly. Sauce can be served warm or chilled.

• Cut angel food cake into 12 slices. To serve, spoon sauce over each slice.

*Makes 12 servings*

**Prep Time:** 10 minutes
**Cook Time:** 5 minutes

# Lemon Chiffon Pie

### ▐▐▐

⅔ cup boiling water
1 package (4-serving size)
   JELL-O® Brand Lemon
   Flavor Gelatin Dessert
2 teaspoons grated lemon
   peel
2 tablespoons lemon juice
½ cup cold water
   Ice cubes
1 tub (8 ounces) COOL WHIP®
   Whipped Topping, thawed
1 prepared graham cracker
   crumb crust (6 ounces)

STIR boiling water into gelatin in large bowl at least 2 minutes or until completely dissolved. Stir in lemon peel and juice. Mix cold water and ice to make 1¼ cups. Add to gelatin, stirring until slightly thickened. Remove any remaining ice.

STIR in whipped topping with wire whisk until smooth. Refrigerate 20 to 30 minutes or until mixture is very thick and will mound. Spoon into crust.

REFRIGERATE 6 hours or overnight until firm. Garnish as desired.          *Makes 8 servings*

**Preparation Time:** 20 minutes
**Refrigerating Time:** 6½ hours

# Cocoa Cappuccino Mousse

### ▐▐▐

1 can (14 ounces) sweetened
   condensed milk (not
   evaporated milk)
⅓ cup HERSHEY'S Cocoa
3 tablespoons butter or
   margarine
2 teaspoons powdered
   instant coffee or
   espresso, dissolved in
   2 teaspoons hot water
2 cups (1 pint) cold whipping
   cream

1. Combine sweetened condensed milk, cocoa, butter and coffee in medium saucepan. Cook over low heat, stirring constantly, until butter melts and mixture is smooth. Remove from heat; cool.

2. Beat whipping cream in large bowl until stiff. Gradually fold chocolate mixture into whipped cream. Spoon into dessert dishes. Refrigerate until set, about 2 hours. Garnish as desired.          *Makes 8 servings*

**Prep Time:** 15 minutes
**Cook Time:** 10 minutes
**Chill Time:** 2 hours

*Lemon Chiffon Pie*

# Pineapple Mousse Torte

▮▮▮

Chocolate Crumb Crust
(recipe follows)
1 package (8 ounces) cream
cheese, softened
1¼ cups sugar
½ teaspoon grated lemon peel
1 can (15¼ ounces) DEL
MONTE® Crushed
Pineapple In Its Own
Juice, undrained
1 can (8 ounces) DEL
MONTE® Pineapple
Tidbits In Its Own Juice,
undrained
2 envelopes unflavored
gelatin
2¼ cups whipping cream,
whipped

1. Prepare crumb crust; set aside.

2. Blend cream cheese with sugar and lemon peel.

3. Drain juice from crushed pineapple and tidbits into small saucepan. Sprinkle gelatin over juice. Place over low heat and stir until gelatin is completely dissolved.

4. Add crushed pineapple to cream cheese mixture; stir in gelatin mixture until blended. Thoroughly fold in whipped cream.

5. Pour filling into crust. Chill at least 5 hours or overnight.

6. Remove sides of pan. Top with pineapple tidbits and garnish, if desired.

*Makes 10 to 12 servings*

**Prep Time:** 20 minutes
**Chill Time:** 5 hours

## CHOCOLATE CRUMB CRUST
2¼ cups chocolate wafer
crumbs
½ cup butter or margarine,
melted

Mix ingredients; press firmly onto bottom of 9-inch springform pan.

## Summer Peach Short "Cakes"

■ ■ ■

**6 medium peaches or
    nectarines, peeled and
    thinly sliced**
**⅓ cup sugar**
**2 tablespoons orange or
    lemon juice**
**⅓ cup chocolate-covered
    toffee pieces**
**1 container (16 ounces)
    cream cheese frosting**
**2 frozen pound cakes
    (10.75 ounces each)**

**1.** Combine peaches, sugar and orange juice in large bowl. Crush peaches with potato masher or large spoon. Stir well; set aside.

**2.** Stir toffee into frosting; set aside. Cut pound cakes into ¼-inch slices; discard end pieces. Spread 1 tablespoon frosting mixture on 1 side of cake slice; top with another slice, pressing gently. Repeat with remaining slices and frosting. To serve, place 2 cake sandwiches on each plate; top each with ¼ cup peach mixture.

*Makes about 7 servings*

**Serving Suggestion:** For a special touch, cut each cake sandwich into triangles and arrange on serving platter in a starburst design. Spoon peach mixture into center.

**Prep Time:** 30 minutes

*Summer Peach Short "Cakes"*

# FROZEN DESSERTS AND ICE CREAM

## Frozen Lime Cheesecake Pie

½ cup milk
½ cup sugar
⅓ cup KARO® Light Corn Syrup
2 teaspoons grated lime peel
¼ cup lime juice
1 package (8 ounces) cream cheese, cut into cubes
1 prepared (9-inch) graham cracker crumb crust
1 cup heavy or whipping cream, whipped
Additional grated lime peel for garnish

**1.** In blender container combine milk, sugar, corn syrup, 2 teaspoons lime peel and juice. Cover and blend on medium speed until smooth.

**2.** With blender running, gradually add cream cheese cubes; blend just until smooth. Pour into crust.

**3.** Freeze several hours or overnight.

**4.** Garnish with whipped cream and additional grated lime peel.
*Makes 8 servings*

**Frozen Lemon Cheesecake Pie:** Prepare Frozen Lime Cheesecake Pie as directed but use ⅔ cup sugar. Substitute 2 teaspoons grated lemon peel and ¼ cup lemon juice for lime peel and lime juice.

*Frozen Lime Cheesecake Pie*

# Italian Ice

### ▮▮▮

**1 cup sweet or dry fruity
 white wine**
**1 cup water**
**1 cup sugar**
**1 cup lemon juice**
**2 egg whites**
 **Fresh berries (optional)**
 **Mint leaves for garnish**

**1.** Place wine and water in small saucepan; add sugar. Cook over medium-high heat until sugar has dissolved and syrup boils, stirring frequently. Cover; boil 1 minute. Uncover; adjust heat to maintain simmer. Simmer 10 minutes without stirring. Remove from heat. Refrigerate 1 hour or until syrup is completely cool.

**2.** Stir lemon juice into cooled syrup. Pour into 9-inch round cake pan. Freeze 1 hour.

**3.** Quickly stir mixture with fork breaking up ice crystals. Freeze 1 hour more or until firm but not solid. Meanwhile, place medium bowl in freezer to chill.

**4.** Beat egg whites in small bowl with electric mixer at high speed until stiff peaks form. Remove lemon ice mixture from cake pan to chilled bowl. Immediately beat ice with whisk or fork until smooth.

**5.** Fold in egg whites; mix well. Spread egg mixture evenly into same cake pan. Freeze 30 minutes. Immediately stir with fork; cover cake pan with foil. Freeze at least 3 hours or until firm.

**6.** To serve, scoop Italian Ice into fluted champagne glasses or dessert dishes. Serve with berries. Garnish, if desired.

*Makes 4 servings*

*Italian Ice*

# Kahlúa® Cappuccino Almond Pie

▮▮▮

1 (9-inch) prepared chocolate cookie or graham cracker crumb crust
1 teaspoon espresso instant coffee powder
6 tablespoons KAHLÚA® Liqueur, divided
2 cups French vanilla or vanilla ice cream, softened
2 cups mocha almond fudge ice cream, softened
3 cups dairy whipped topping
¼ cup toasted sliced almonds
Heavenly Kahlúa® Fudge Sauce (recipe follows)

Place crust in freezer. Stir coffee powder and 2 tablespoons Kahlúa® into softened vanilla ice cream until well mixed. Remove crust from freezer. Spoon ice cream mixture quickly into crust; freeze until firm. Stir 2 tablespoons Kahlúa® into mocha almond fudge ice cream; spoon over vanilla layer. Freeze until firm. Stir remaining 2 tablespoons Kahlúa® into whipped topping until blended. Spread over top of pie; sprinkle with almonds just before serving. Serve with Heavenly Kahlúa® Fudge Sauce.

*Makes 1 (9-inch) pie*

## HEAVENLY KAHLÚA® FUDGE SAUCE

1 (16-ounce) can chocolate fudge topping
¼ cup KAHLÚA® Liqueur

In saucepan (or microwavable bowl), heat fudge topping (or microwave at HIGH) until melted; stir in Kahlúa®. Serve warm. To store, cover and refrigerate; reheat as needed.

*Makes 1⅔ cups*

# Champagne Sorbet

▮▮▮

¼ cup sugar
1 envelope unflavored gelatin
½ cup water
2½ cups white champagne
1 cup KARO® Light Corn Syrup
2 tablespoons lemon juice
Raspberry Sauce (recipe follows)
Fresh berries (optional)

**1.** In 3-quart saucepan mix sugar and gelatin. Stir in water; let stand 1 minute. Stirring constantly, cook over low heat 5 minutes or until gelatin is dissolved; remove from heat.

**2.** Stir in champagne, corn syrup and lemon juice until smooth. Pour into 8- or 9-inch square baking pan. Cover; freeze until firm.

**3.** Spoon frozen champagne mixture into chilled large bowl. With mixer at low speed, beat until smooth but not melted. Pour into pan or freezer container. Cover; freeze until firm.

**4.** Scoop into serving glasses. Top with Raspberry Sauce. If desired, garnish with fresh berries.        *Makes 12 servings*

**Raspberry Sauce:** In blender or food processor, purée 1 package (10 ounces) frozen raspberries in syrup. Press through fine strainer into bowl to remove seeds. Stir in ⅓ cup KARO® Light Corn Syrup.
       *Makes 1¼ cups*

# Mud Pie

▎ ▎ ▎

1¼ cups chocolate graham
    cracker crumbs
3 tablespoons sugar
¼ cup Prune Purée (recipe
    follows) or prepared
    prune butter
1 quart fat-free coffee ice
    cream or frozen yogurt
1 cup prepared fat-free fudge
    sauce
½ cup low-fat nondairy
    whipped topping

Preheat oven to 375°F. Coat 9-inch pie plate with vegetable cooking spray. In large bowl, mix crumbs and sugar. Cut in prune purée until mixture resembles coarse crumbs. Press onto bottom and side of prepared pie plate. Bake in center of oven 15 minutes. Cool completely. Soften ice cream slightly. Spoon evenly into pie shell. Freeze until firm. Cover ice cream with fudge sauce. Cut into wedges and serve immediately or cover and return to freezer for up to 1 week before serving. Top each serving with 1 tablespoon whipped topping.
       *Makes 8 servings*

**Prune Purée:** Combine 1⅓ cups (8 ounces) pitted prunes and 6 tablespoons hot water in container of food processor or blender. Pulse on and off until prunes are finely chopped and smooth. Store leftovers in covered container in refrigerator for up to two months.
       *Makes 1 cup*

*Favorite recipe from* **California Prune Board**

# Citus Sorbet

■ ■ ■

**1 can (12 ounces) DOLE®
Orange Peach Mango or
Tropical Fruit Frozen
Juice Concentrate
1 can (8 ounces) DOLE®
Crushed Pineapple or
Pineapple Tidbits, drained
½ cup plain nonfat or low-fat
yogurt
2½ cups cold water**

• Combine frozen juice concentrate, pineapple and yogurt in blender or food processor container; blend until smooth. Stir in water.

• Pour mixture into container of ice cream maker.* Freeze according to manufacturer's directions.

*Makes 10 servings*

*\*Or, pour sorbet mixture into 8-inch square metal pan; cover. Freeze 1½ to 2 hours or until slightly firm. Place in large bowl; beat with electric mixer on medium speed 1 minute or until slushy. Return mixture to metal pan; repeat freezing and beating steps. Freeze until firm, about 6 hours or overnight.*

**Passion-Banana Sorbet:**
Substitute DOLE® Pine-Orange-Banana Frozen Juice Concentrate for frozen juice concentrate. Prepare sorbet as directed above except reduce water to 2 cups and omit canned pineapple.

# Caramel Sundae

■ ■ ■

**1 cup low-fat (1%) milk
1 tablespoon cornstarch
½ cup firmly packed dark
brown sugar
1 tablespoon margarine
1 teaspoon vanilla
1 pint vanilla ice milk or
nonfat frozen yogurt,
divided**

**1.** Combine milk and cornstarch in heavy saucepan. Stir until cornstarch is completely dissolved. Add brown sugar and margarine; cook over medium-low heat, stirring constantly with wire whisk. Bring to a boil. Boil 1 minute. Remove from heat; stir in vanilla. Cool to room temperature.

**2.** Place ½ cup ice milk in each of four sherbet glasses. Top each with ¼ cup caramel sauce.

*Makes 4 servings*

*Caramel Sundae*

# KITCHEN TOOL TIME ICE CREAM MAKER

Homemade ice cream, when properly made, is smooth and creamy with fine ice crystals. For best results, carefully read the manufacturer's directions for the ice cream maker. Homemade ice cream develops large ice crystals after two or three days, resulting in a coarse texture, so try to eat it within a day or two of making it.

There are three basic types of ice cream makers: bucket models, cylinder freezers and self-cooling units.

## • Bucket Model

This classic machine uses salt and ice to cool the ice cream container. They can be electric or manual operating, requiring you to crank the motor for churning the ice cream.

## • Cylinder Freezer

The container on these types is surrounded by a layer of coolant that is liquid at room temperature and freezes when placed in your freezer for several hours. These too can be electric or manual operating.

## • Self-Cooling

Expensive and large, these are the easiest makers to use and generally produce the best results. All you need to do is add your ice cream mixture and push a button.

The following tips will help produce smooth, creamy homemade ice cream:

• Thoroughly chill the ice cream mixture before freezing it to ensure a smooth texture. Chilling also cuts freezing time.

• Fill the canister no more than two-thirds full to allow the mixture to expand.

• The ice cream mixture must be constantly stirred during the freezing process.

• After freezing, the ice cream needs to stand for at least four hours to develop flavor. This can be done in the ice cream maker by packing it with additional ice and salt (4 cups ice to 1 cup salt—the higher proportion of salt lowers the temperature of the ice cream). The alternative method is to transfer the ice cream to a covered freezer container and place it in a 0°F freezer.

# Avocado Ice Cream

4 cups milk
1 cup sugar, divided
1 vanilla bean*
2 whole eggs
1 egg yolk
3 ripe avocados, peeled and
    pitted
¼ cup fresh lime juice

*Or, substitute 1½ teaspoons vanilla for vanilla bean. Add to milk in step 1. Omit step 2.*

**1.** Combine milk, ¾ cup sugar and vanilla bean in medium saucepan. Cook and stir over medium-high heat just until milk begins to boil; remove from heat.

**2.** Cut vanilla bean in half lengthwise. Scrape seeds into saucepan; add bean halves to saucepan.

**3.** Combine remaining ¼ cup sugar, whole eggs and egg yolk in large bowl. Beat mixture until frothy and light lemon color. Continue whisking mixture while very slowly pouring in 1 cup hot milk mixture.

**4.** Slowly pour egg mixture into saucepan with vanilla bean. Cook over medium heat and whisk slowly until first bubble forms. *Do not boil.*

**5.** Pour custard mixture through fine-meshed sieve into medium bowl set in ice water; stir custard mixture until cool. Cover and refrigerate about 1 hour or until cold.

**6.** Combine avocados and lime juice in medium bowl. Mash with wooden spoon or potato masher. Press avocado mixture through fine-meshed strainer with rubber spatula; stir into custard mixture.

**7.** Freeze in ice cream maker according to manufacturer's directions.
*Makes about 1½ quarts*

*Avocado Ice Cream*

# Frozen Brandy Cream in Brandy Lace Cups

▌▌▌

**4 egg yolks**
**⅓ cup KARO® Light Corn Syrup**
**⅓ cup sugar**
**2 tablespoons brandy***
**1 cup heavy or whipping cream**
**Brandy Lace Cups (recipe follows)**

*Or, use 2 tablespoons orange juice plus ½ teaspoon grated orange peel.*

**1.** In small bowl with mixer at high speed, beat egg yolks until light and fluffy, about 10 minutes.

**2.** Meanwhile, in 1-quart saucepan combine corn syrup and sugar. Stirring frequently, bring to full boil over medium heat. Without stirring, boil 2 minutes or until temperature on candy thermometer reaches 240°F.

**3.** Beating constantly, gradually pour hot syrup in thin, steady stream into egg yolk mixture. Continue beating until thick and completely cool, about 20 minutes. Gently fold in brandy.

**4.** In chilled mixer bowl beat cream until stiff. Lightly fold about half of brandy mixture into whipped cream.

**5.** Gently fold in remaining brandy mixture. Cover; freeze 4 to 5 hours or overnight.

**6.** Just before serving, spoon into Brandy Lace Cups. If desired, garnish each cup with fruit.          *Makes about 2½ cups*

## BRANDY LACE CUPS

**¼ cup KARO® Light or Dark Corn Syrup**
**¼ cup (½ stick) MAZOLA® Margarine or butter**
**¼ cup sugar**
**½ cup all-purpose flour**
**¼ cup very finely chopped pecans or walnuts**
**2 tablespoons brandy**
**1 ounce semisweet chocolate, melted (optional)**

**1.** Preheat oven to 350°F. Grease 2 (15½×12-inch) cookie sheets.

**2.** In small saucepan combine corn syrup, margarine and sugar. Stirring constantly, bring to full boil over medium heat. Remove from heat. Stir in flour, nuts and brandy.

**3.** Drop 4 rounded tablespoons of batter about 7 inches apart onto each prepared cookie sheet.

**4.** Bake 6 to 8 minutes or until golden. Cool on cookie sheet 1 minute or until cookies can be lifted from sheet but are still pliable.

**5.** Remove cookies with spatula; drape shiny-side down over bottom of drinking glass or 6-ounce custard cup, pressing gently to form cups. If cookies harden before shaping, reheat briefly on cookie sheet.

**6.** Cool cups completely. Store in airtight container. If desired, drizzle cups with melted chocolate just before filling.

*Makes 8 to 10 dessert cups*

# French Vanilla Freeze

▌▌▌

10¾ teaspoons EQUAL® FOR RECIPES *or* 36 packets EQUAL® sweetener *or* 1½ cups EQUAL® SPOONFUL™
2 tablespoons cornstarch
1 piece vanilla bean (2 inches)
⅛ teaspoon salt
2 cups skim milk
2 tablespoons margarine
1 cup real liquid egg product
1 teaspoon vanilla

• Combine Equal®, cornstarch, vanilla bean and salt in medium saucepan; stir in milk and margarine. Heat to boiling over medium-high heat, whisking constantly. Boil until thickened, whisking constantly, about 1 minute.

• Whisk about 1 cup milk mixture into egg product in small bowl; whisk egg mixture back into milk mixture in saucepan. Cook over very low heat, whisking constantly, 30 to 60 seconds. Remove from heat and stir in vanilla. Let cool; remove vanilla bean. Refrigerate until chilled, about 1 hour.

• Freeze mixture in ice cream maker according to manufacturer's directions. Pack into freezer container and freeze until firm, 8 hours or overnight. Before serving, let stand at room temperature until slightly softened, about 15 minutes.

*Makes 6 (½-cup) servings*

## Cook's Notes

The flavor of vanilla beans is highly superior to the flavor of vanilla extract. The beans are actually seed pods of a certain variety of orchid and the vanilla essence lies inside the beans in hundreds of tiny black seeds.

# Baker's® Frozen Black Bottom Pie

**1 cup Regal Chocolate Sauce (recipe follows)**
**1 prepared chocolate crumb crust (9-inch)**
**1 quart ice cream, any flavor, softened**
**Chocolate cookie crumbs**

**POUR** Regal Chocolate Sauce into crust, spreading over sides and bottom. Refrigerate.

**FILL** crust with ice cream. Garnish with chocolate cookie crumbs. Freeze until firm, about 2 hours.

*Makes 8 servings*

**Regal Chocolate Sauce:**
Microwave 2 squares BAKER'S® Unsweetened Baking Chocolate and ⅓ cup water in large microwavable bowl on HIGH 1½ minutes. Stir until chocolate is completely melted. Stir in ½ cup sugar and 1 tablespoon MAXWELL HOUSE® Instant Coffee, any variety. Microwave 1 minute. Stir. Microwave 2 minutes. Stir in 3 tablespoons butter or margarine and ¼ teaspoon vanilla.  Makes about 1 cup

**Prep Time:** 20 minutes
**Freeze Time:** 2 hours

# Easy Orange Ice Cream

**2 cups heavy cream or whipping cream**
**1 cup sugar**
**⅓ cup fresh squeezed lemon juice**
**Grated peel of 1 SUNKIST® Orange**
**⅓ cup fresh squeezed orange juice**

In large bowl, combine cream and sugar; stir to dissolve sugar. Add lemon juice; continue stirring. (Mixture will thicken slightly.) Stir in orange peel and juice. Pour into shallow pan; freeze until firm, about 4 hours. Serve in dessert dishes.

*Makes 6 servings*

*Baker's® Frozen Black Bottom Pie*

# Strawberry-Banana Granité

###

2 ripe bananas, peeled and
  sliced (about 2 cups)
2 cups unsweetened frozen
  strawberries *(do not
  thaw)*
¼ cup no-sugar-added
  strawberry pourable fruit*
  Whole fresh strawberries
  (optional)
  Fresh mint leaves (optional)

*\*3 tablespoons no-sugar-added
strawberry fruit spread combined with
1 tablespoon warm water may be
substituted.*

Place banana slices in plastic
bag; freeze until firm. Place
frozen banana slices and frozen
strawberries in food processor
container. Let stand 10 minutes
for fruit to soften slightly. Add
pourable fruit. Remove plunger
from top of food processor to
allow air to be incorporated.
Process until smooth, scraping
down sides of container
frequently. Serve immediately.
Garnish with fresh strawberries
and mint leaves, if desired.
Freeze leftovers.

*Makes 5 servings*

# Cool 'n Creamy Chocolate Pie

###

1 package (3 ounces) cream
  cheese, softened
¼ cup sugar
1 teaspoon vanilla extract
½ cup HERSHEY'S Syrup
1 cup cold whipping cream
1 packaged crumb crust
  (6 ounces)
  Sliced fresh fruit (optional)
  Chocolate curls (optional)

**1.** Beat cream cheese, sugar
and vanilla in medium bowl
until well blended. Gradually
add syrup, beating until
smooth. Beat whipping cream
until stiff. Carefully fold into
chocolate mixture. Pour into
crust.

**2.** Cover; freeze until firm,
about 3 hours. Just before
serving, garnish with fresh fruit
and chocolate curls, if desired.
*Makes 6 to 8 servings*

## Ice Cream Sandwich Hearts

▌▌▌

1 box (21.1 ounces) blondie
    brownie mix with walnuts
2 eggs
¼ cup oil
3 cups chocolate or vanilla
    ice cream, softened
Chocolate sauce

**1.** Preheat oven to 350°F. Grease 15×10-inch jelly-roll pan.

**2.** Prepare blondie mix according to package directions with eggs, oil and 2 tablespoons water. Spread batter evenly in prepared pan.

**3.** Bake 15 to 20 minutes or until toothpick inserted in center comes out clean. Blondies should be soft. *Do not overbake.* Cool completely in pan. Cover with plastic wrap; set aside up to 2 days.

**4.** To complete recipe, cut 12 heart-shaped cookies from blondies with 3- or 4-inch cookie cutter. (Reserve scraps for snacking or discard.) Spoon ¼ cup ice cream onto cookie. Top with another cookie, pressing gently to spread ice cream to edges. Scrape excess ice cream from edges. To serve, place sandwiches on plates and drizzle with chocolate sauce.

*Makes 12 servings*

## Apple-Lemon Sherbet

▌▌▌

1 (16-ounce) jar MOTT'S®
    Apple Sauce
½ cup frozen apple juice
    concentrate, thawed
¼ cup lemon juice
1 egg white*

*\*Use clean, uncracked egg.*

**1.** In food processor or blender, process apple sauce until smooth. Add juice concentrate, lemon juice and egg white; process until frothy.

**2.** Pour into ice cream maker freezer container; freeze according to manufacturer's directions. Or, pour into 8- or 9-inch square pan. Cover; freeze about 2 hours or until almost firm. Transfer to food processor or blender; process until smooth. *Makes 8 servings*

# Strawberry Margarita Pie

■ ■ ■

1 package (8 ounces) frozen
  sweetened whole
  strawberries, thawed
1 package (8 ounces) cream
  cheese, cubed
1½ tablespoons lime juice
2 teaspoons tequila
½ teaspoon freshly grated
  orange peel
4 ounces frozen whipped
  topping, thawed
1 (10-inch) graham cracker
  crumb pie crust, chilled

In blender or food processor combine strawberries, cream cheese, lime juice, tequila and orange peel. Blend or process until combined. Pour mixture into medium bowl; fold in whipped topping. Gently pour into pie crust. Freeze until firm, 4 to 6 hours or overnight. Let stand at room temperature 5 minutes before serving.

*Makes 8 to 10 servings*

**Serving Suggestion:** Garnish with fresh strawberry slices and mint leaves.

*Favorite recipe from* **Lawry's®**

# Honey Frozen Yogurt

■ ■ ■

2 cups 2% low-fat milk
¾ cup honey
  Dash salt
2 eggs, beaten
2 cups plain low-fat yogurt
1 tablespoon vanilla

Heat milk in large saucepan over medium-low heat. *Do not boil.* Stir in honey and salt. Pour small amount of milk mixture into eggs; return to remaining milk mixture in saucepan. Cook and stir over medium-low heat 5 minutes or until mixture coats back of wooden spoon. *Do not boil.* Remove from heat and cool completely. Stir in yogurt and vanilla. Refrigerate until cold. Turn into 13×9×2-inch metal pan. Freeze until firm, stirring every 20 to 30 minutes or freeze in ice cream maker according to manufacturer's directions.      *Makes 1 quart*

*Favorite recipe from* **National Honey Board**

# Caribbean Freeze

⅔ cup sugar
3 tablespoons HERSHEY'S Cocoa
1¾ cups water
3 tablespoons frozen pineapple juice concentrate, thawed
1 tablespoon golden rum *or*
½ teaspoon rum extract

**1.** Stir together sugar and cocoa in medium saucepan; stir in water. Cook over medium heat, stirring occasionally, until mixture comes to a boil. Reduce heat; simmer 3 minutes, stirring occasionally. Cool completely.

**2.** Stir concentrate and rum into chocolate mixture. Cover; refrigerate until cold, about 6 hours.

**3.** Pour cold mixture into 1-quart ice cream freezer. Freeze according to manufacturer's directions. Garnish as desired.
   *Makes 6 servings (¾ cups each)*

*Caribbean Freeze*

# Smoothies and summer refreshers

## California Shake

■■■

¾ cup DOLE® Pitted Dates, halved
1 medium, ripe DOLE® Banana, quartered
1 cup fat-free or low-fat frozen vanilla yogurt, slightly softened
½ cup low-fat or nonfat milk

• Combine dates and banana in blender or food processor container. Blend until dates are finely chopped.

• Add yogurt and milk; blend until thick and smooth. Serve immediately. Garnish with banana slices, if desired.

*Makes 2 servings*

## Pineberry Smoothie

■■■

1 ripe DOLE® Banana, quartered
1 cup DOLE® Pineapple Juice
½ cup nonfat vanilla or plain yogurt
½ cup fresh or frozen strawberries, raspberries or blueberries

• Combine all ingredients in blender or food processor container. Blend until thick and smooth. Serve immediately.

*Makes 2 servings*

*Clockwise from top: California Shake, Pineberry Smoothie and Fuzzy Banana Navel (page 68)*

## Fat-Free Honey Berry Milkshakes

▌▌▌

2½ cups strawberries or assorted berries
1 pint nonfat vanilla frozen yogurt or ice cream
½ cup nonfat milk
¼ cup honey
4 small mint sprigs

Combine all ingredients except mint sprigs in blender or food processor; process about 30 seconds or until smooth. Pour into tall glasses. Garnish with mint sprigs. *Makes 4 cups*

*Favorite recipe from* **National Honey Board**

## Honey Lemonade with Frozen Fruit Cubes

▌▌▌

1½ cups lemon juice
¾ cup honey
9 cups water
48 small pieces assorted fruit

Combine lemon juice and honey in large pitcher; stir until honey is dissolved. Stir in water. Place 1 to 2 pieces of fruit in each compartment of 2 ice cube trays. Fill each compartment with honey lemonade and freeze until firm. Chill remaining lemonade. To serve, divide frozen fruit cubes between tall glasses and fill with remaining lemonade.
*Makes 9 cups*

*Favorite recipe from* **National Honey Board**

## Cooler-than-Cool Yogurt Drink

▌▌▌

2 cups plain yogurt
1 small ripe avocado, pitted, peeled and diced
⅔ cup cubed seeded peeled cucumber
5 to 6 fresh mint leaves *or* ½ teaspoon dried mint leaves
½ teaspoon celery salt
½ teaspoon TABASCO® brand Pepper Sauce
1 cup cracked ice

Combine all ingredients in blender. Cover; process until smooth. Garnish with additional mint, if desired.
*Makes 4 servings*

*Left to right: Fat-Free Honey Berry Milkshakes and Honey Lemonade with Frozen Fruit Cubes*

# Choco-Berry Cooler

### ▐▐▐

¾ cup cold milk
¼ cup sliced fresh strawberries
2 tablespoons HERSHEY'S Syrup
2 tablespoons plus 2 small scoops vanilla ice cream, divided
  Cold ginger ale or club soda
  Fresh strawberry
  Mint leaves (optional)

**1.** Place milk, strawberries, chocolate syrup and 2 tablespoons ice cream in blender container. Cover and blend until smooth.

**2.** Alternate remaining 2 scoops ice cream and chocolate mixture in tall ice cream glass; fill glass with ginger ale. Garnish with fresh strawberry and mint leaves, if desired. Serve immediately.

*Makes one 14-ounce serving*

**Variations:** Before blending, substitute one of the following fruits for fresh strawberries: 3 tablespoons frozen strawberries with syrup, thawed; ½ peeled fresh peach *or* ⅓ cup canned peach slices; 2 slices canned *or* ¼ cup canned crushed pineapple; or ¼ cup sweetened fresh raspberries *or* 3 tablespoons frozen raspberries with syrup, thawed.

# Valentine Smoothie

### ▐▐▐

1 cup vanilla low-fat yogurt
1 ripe banana, sliced
2 tablespoons strawberry jam
1 tablespoon honey or granulated sugar
3 or 4 drops red food coloring

Combine yogurt, banana, jam, honey and food coloring in blender container; cover. Blend on high 20 seconds or until foamy. Pour into 2 glasses; serve immediately. Garnish as desired.     *Makes 2 servings*

# Fuzzy Banana Navel

### ▐▐▐

2 medium, ripe DOLE® Bananas, quartered
1 pint orange sorbet or orange sherbet, slightly softened
1 cup DOLE® Orange Peach Mango Juice

Combine bananas, sorbet and juice in blender or food processor. Blend until thick and smooth. Garnish with orange slices and curls, if desired. Serve immediately.

*Makes 4 servings*

# Berries, Berries, Berries!

## Fantasy in Berries

**III**

1 bag (12 ounces) frozen
    unsweetened raspberries,
    thawed
¼ cup plus 2 tablespoons
    sugar, divided
1 tablespoon fresh lemon juice
2 cups sliced fresh
    strawberries
1 cup fresh raspberries
1 cup fresh blueberries
1 cup low-fat ricotta cheese
1 teaspoon vanilla extract
¼ teaspoon almond extract

**1.** Place thawed frozen raspberries, ¼ cup sugar and lemon juice in blender or food processor; blend until smooth. Pour through strainer to remove seeds. Spoon 3 tablespoons raspberry sauce on each of 8 plates. Tilt each plate, rotating to spread raspberry sauce over bottom of plate.

**2.** Arrange ¼ cup sliced strawberries, 2 tablespoons fresh raspberries and 2 tablespoons fresh blueberries on top of sauce in desired pattern on each plate.

**3.** Place cheese, remaining 2 tablespoons sugar and vanilla and almond extracts in clean blender or food processor; blend until smooth and satiny.

**4.** Spoon cheese mixture into pastry bag and pipe onto berries, using about 2 tablespoons per serving. (Use star tip to make rosettes or various sizes of writing tips to drizzle mixture over berries.) Before serving, garnish with mint sprigs and edible flowers, such as pansies, violets or nasturtiums, if desired.

*Makes 8 servings*

# Three-Berry Kuchen

**▌▌▌**

1¾ cups all-purpose flour, divided
2 teaspoons baking powder
½ teaspoon baking soda
½ teaspoon salt
⅔ cup MOTT'S® Apple Sauce
4 egg whites
¼ cup nonfat plain yogurt
2 tablespoons granulated sugar
1 teaspoon grated lemon peel
2 cups assorted blueberries, raspberries or blackberries
¼ cup light brown sugar
2 tablespoons margarine

**1.** Preheat oven to 350°F. Spray 10-inch round cake pan with nonstick cooking spray. In small bowl, combine 1½ cups flour, baking powder, baking soda and salt.

**2.** In large bowl, whisk together apple sauce, egg whites, yogurt, granulated sugar and lemon peel. Add flour mixture; stir until well blended. Spread batter into prepared pan.

**3.** Sprinkle berries over batter. Combine remaining ¼ cup flour and brown sugar in small bowl. Cut in margarine with pastry blender or fork until mixture resembles coarse crumbs. Sprinkle over berries.

**4.** Bake 50 to 55 minutes or until lightly browned. Cool on wire rack 20 minutes. Serve warm or cool completely.

*Makes 9 servings*

# Philadelphia® 3-Step® Midwest Cheesecake

**▌▌▌**

2 packages (8 ounces each) PHILADELPHIA® Cream Cheese, softened
½ cup sugar
½ teaspoon vanilla
2 eggs
1 (9-inch) ready-to-use graham cracker crust
½ cup sour cream
3 cups whole strawberries, stems removed
2 tablespoons strawberry jelly, heated

**1. MIX** cream cheese, sugar and vanilla at medium speed with electric mixer until well blended. Add eggs; mix until blended.

**2. POUR** into crust.

**3. BAKE** at 350°F, 40 minutes or until center is almost set. Cool. Refrigerate 3 hours or overnight. Spread sour cream over cheesecake. Top with strawberries, stem-side down. Drizzle with jelly.

*Makes 8 servings*

*Philadelphia® 3-Step® Midwest Cheesecake*

# THE FRESH REPORT

*Although available virtually year-round, berries are at their peak in summertime. Four of the most common berries are strawberries, blueberries, raspberries and blackberries.*

## STRAWBERRIES

*Availability:* California strawberries are in season about 10 months of the year, taking a brief hiatus in December and January. Florida berries are available from January to May. With Chilean and Mexican crops filling in the gap during winter months, there is an uninterrupted supply. In most of the United States, locally grown berries reach the market in May and June.

*Buying Tips:* Look for berries that are shiny, bright red and fragrant. The green caps should be vibrant and the berries should be reasonably clean.

*Storage:* Strawberries can be refrigerated, unwashed, for up to three days.

## BLACKBERRIES

*Availability:* The season extends from May through August. Oregon, Washington, Michigan, New Jersey, Texas, Oklahoma and Arkansas are large domestic producers. Winter supplies come from Chile and New Zealand.

*Buying Tips:* Select plump berries that are glossy, almost black in color and feel slightly soft. Hard berries are probably not fully ripe and will be quite tart.

*Storage:* Blackberries are highly perishable and should be refrigerated only for a day or two in the original container or spread in a single layer in a pan and covered with a damp paper towel. Before storing them, discard any moldy berries.

# RASPBERRIES

*Availability:* Summer is the prime season for domestic raspberries. Winter supplies come from Chile and New Zealand.

*Buying Tips:* Plump berries that have a rich color and a sweet, berrylike aroma are apt to be sweet and luscious. Avoid berries that have a hull attached in the center. This is a sign that they were picked before fully ripening and they are likely to be tart.

*Storage:* Raspberries are extremely perishable. Buy small quantities and plan on using them within a day or two. Never wash berries before storing. Remove any crushed berries, because they will mold quickly. Store in the refrigerator.

# BLUEBERRIES

*Availability:* A blueberry bush has a short harvest season. However, blueberries are now grown from Florida to Canada, keeping supermarkets supplied with fresh berries from May to September. If you live in an area where blueberries are grown, you will find them in abundance during their short peak season at produce and farmers' markets.

*Buying Tips:* Choose firm, plump berries with a silvery bloom. Avoid shriveled blueberries or berries with a green or red tint (an indication of an underripe berry).

*Storage:* If packaged in plastic, fresh blueberries should be stored in the refrigerator in their original package. If packaged in cardboard, the blueberries should be transferred to an airtight container. Fresh berries may be kept up to ten days.

# Smucker's® Chilled Berry Soup

### ▌▌▌

3 cups fresh blueberries
2 cups fresh raspberries
½ cup SMUCKER'S®
    Strawberry Jelly
Juice of 1 lemon
1½ cups water, divided
1 teaspoon cornstarch
    dissolved in 2 tablespoons
    cold water
1 quart fresh strawberries,
    cleaned and sliced
1 cup plain nonfat yogurt or
    sour cream

In a large saucepan, combine blueberries, raspberries, jelly, lemon juice and 1 cup water. Bring to a boil; simmer about 5 minutes or until blueberries begin to lose some of their juice. Stir in cornstarch mixture; cook until slightly thickened, about 3 more minutes. Add remaining ½ cup water. Cool; refrigerate berry mixture until thoroughly chilled.

Place chilled berry mixture in blender or food processor. Blend on low speed 5 minutes. Combine puréed berry soup with sliced strawberries. Spoon into serving bowls; stir a few tablespoons yogurt into each serving.

*Makes 6 (1-cup) servings*

# Chilean Raspberry and Blueberry Pie

### ▌▌▌

Pastry for 2-crust, 9-inch pie
    (homemade or prepared)
1⅓ cups plus 1 teaspoon sugar
7 tablespoons cornstarch
1 tablespoon grated orange
    peel
4 cups Chilean raspberries
2 cups Chilean blueberries
1 tablespoon orange liqueur
    *or* ½ teaspoon grated
    orange peel

Preheat oven to 375°F. Line 9-inch pie pan with pastry. Mix 1⅓ cups sugar, cornstarch and orange peel in bowl; add raspberries, blueberries and orange liqueur. Mix well and pour into pie shell. Cover with top crust. Seal edges and flute or press together with tines of fork. Cut slits for steam to escape. Brush lightly with cold water; sprinkle with remaining 1 teaspoon sugar. Bake until top is golden brown, about 50 minutes. Let cool before serving with slightly sweetened whipped cream.

*Makes 8 servings*

*Favorite recipe from* **Chilean Fresh Fruit Association**

# Three-Berry Tart

### ▮▮▮

2 cups all-purpose flour
5 tablespoons unsalted butter
¼ cup ground almonds
⅓ plus ½ cup sifted
    confectioners' sugar
5 tablespoons ice water
1 tablespoon cornstarch
⅓ cup 2% low fat milk
1 cup (4 ounces) shredded
    ALPINE LACE® Reduced
    Sodium Muenster Cheese
1½ cups low fat sour cream
1 cup vanilla nonfat yogurt
1 tablespoon vanilla extract
1 teaspoon grated lemon rind
2 cups strawberries, hulled
    and halved
1½ cups fresh raspberries
1½ cups fresh blueberries
1 cup peeled kiwi slices
½ cup red currant jelly

**1.** To make the almond crust: Preheat the oven to 400°F. In a medium-size bowl, mix the flour, butter, almonds and the ⅓ cup of confectioners' sugar with your fingers until coarse crumbs form. Add enough water to form a dough. Press onto the bottom and up the side of a 12-inch tart pan with a removable bottom. Prick the dough at ½-inch intervals with the tines of a fork and bake for 15 minutes or until golden brown.

**2.** Meanwhile, to make the cheese filling: In a small saucepan, dissolve the cornstarch in the milk. Stir in the cheese and cook over medium heat until the mixture is slightly thickened and smooth. Cool for 15 minutes.

**3.** In a medium-size bowl, with an electric mixer set on medium-high, beat the sour cream, yogurt, the ½ cup of confectioners' sugar, the vanilla and lemon rind for 1 minute. With the mixer running, slowly add the cheese mixture and beat until the filling is almost smooth. Pour into the tart shell and refrigerate for 30 minutes or until filling is thickened and cold.

**4.** To make the fresh fruit topping: Arrange the berries and kiwi decoratively on top of the filling. In a small saucepan, melt the jelly over low heat, then carefully brush over the berries. Refrigerate for at least 1 hour before serving.

*Makes 16 servings*

*Three-Berry Tart*

## Snackin' Banana Split

- **1 ripe small banana, peeled**
- **1 small scoop vanilla nonfat or low-fat frozen yogurt**
- **1 small scoop strawberry nonfat or low-fat frozen yogurt**
- **⅓ cup sliced fresh strawberries or blueberries**
- **2 tablespoons no-sugar-added strawberry fruit spread**
- **1 teaspoon hot water**
- **2 tablespoons low-fat granola cereal**
- **1 maraschino cherry (optional)**

**1.** Split banana in half lengthwise. Place in shallow bowl; top with frozen yogurt and strawberries.

**2.** Combine fruit spread and water in small bowl; mix well. Spoon over yogurt; sprinkle with granola. Top with cherry, if desired.

*Makes 1 serving*

# Cheery Chocolate Animal Cookies

1⅔ cups (10-ounce package) REESE'S® Peanut Butter Chips
1 cup HERSHEY'S Semi-Sweet Chocolate Chips
2 tablespoons shortening (*do not use butter, margarine or oil*)
1 package (20 ounces) chocolate sandwich cookies
1 package (11 ounces) animal crackers

**1.** Line trays or cookie sheets with waxed paper.

**2.** Combine peanut butter chips, chocolate chips and shortening in 2-quart glass measuring cup with handle. Microwave on HIGH (100% power) 1½ to 2 minutes or until chips are melted and mixture is smooth when stirred. Using fork, dip each cookie into melted chip mixture; gently tap fork on side of cup to remove excess chocolate.

**3.** Place coated cookies on prepared trays; top each cookie with 1 animal cracker. Chill until chocolate is set, about 30 minutes. Store in airtight container in cool, dry place.
*Makes about 4 dozen cookies*

# Funny Face Fruit Pizzas

3 tablespoons sugar
1 teaspoon ground cinnamon
6 (6-inch) flour tortillas
2 tablespoons water
1 package (1 ounce) instant sugar-free vanilla pudding (4 servings)
1 DOLE® Banana, sliced
½ DOLE® Mango, peeled, sliced
1 DOLE® Kiwi fruit, peeled, sliced
DOLE® Seedless Raisins (optional)
DOLE® Strawberries (optional)

• Combine sugar and cinnamon. Brush tortillas lightly with water. Sprinkle sugar mixture on top of tortillas.

• Place tortillas on baking sheet sprayed with vegetable cooking spray. Bake at 400°F, 10 minutes or until lightly browned.

• Prepare pudding according to package directions.

• Spoon about ⅓ cup pudding onto each tortilla. Arrange banana, mango, kiwi, raisins and strawberries on pudding to make a funny face or design.
*Makes 6 servings*

*Cheery Chocolate Animal Cookies*

# Frozen Chocolate-Covered Bananas

**2 ripe medium bananas**
**4 wooden sticks**
**½ cup low-fat granola cereal without raisins**
**⅓ cup hot fudge sauce, at room temperature**

**1.** Cover baking sheet or 15×10-inch jelly-roll pan with waxed paper; set aside.

**2.** Peel bananas; cut each in half crosswise. Insert wooden stick into center of cut end of each banana about 1½ inches into banana half. Place on prepared baking sheet; freeze until firm, at least 2 hours.

**3.** Place granola in large plastic food storage bag; crush slightly using rolling pin or meat mallet. Transfer granola to shallow plate. Place fudge sauce in shallow dish.

**4.** Working with 1 banana at a time, place frozen banana in fudge sauce; turn banana and spread fudge sauce evenly onto banana with small rubber scraper. Immediately place banana on plate with granola; turn to coat lightly. Return to baking sheet in freezer. Repeat with remaining bananas.

**5.** Freeze until fudge sauce is very firm, at least 2 hours. Place on small plates; let stand 5 minutes before serving.

*Makes 4 servings*

# Chipwiches

**3 cups any flavor ice cream, sherbet, frozen yogurt or whipped topping**
**24 CHIPS AHOY!® Chocolate Chip Cookies**
**Sprinkles, chocolate chips, chopped nuts, toasted or tinted coconut, or other assorted small candies**

Spread ice cream about ¾ inch thick on flat side of 1 cookie. Place another cookie on top. Roll or lightly press edges in sprinkles. Repeat. Freeze until firm, about 4 hours.

*Makes 12 servings*

**Peanut Butter Chipwiches:** Spread about 1 tablespoon peanut butter on flat side of each of 2 Chips Ahoy!® Cookies. Place banana slice in center of peanut butter on 1 cookie; top with other cookie, peanut butter side down. Continue as above.

*Frozen Chocolate-Covered Bananas*

# The Original Rice Krispies Treats® Recipe

3 tablespoons margarine
1 package (10 ounces, about 40) regular marshmallows *or* 4 cups miniature marshmallows
6 cups KELLOGG'S® RICE KRISPIES® cereal
Vegetable cooking spray

**1.** Melt margarine in large saucepan over low heat. Add marshmallows and stir until completely melted. Remove from heat.

**2.** Add Kellogg's® Rice Krispies® cereal. Stir until well coated.

**3.** Using buttered spatula or waxed paper, press mixture evenly into 13×9×2-inch pan coated with cooking spray. Cut into 2×2-inch squares when cool.
   *Makes 24 (2-inch-square) treats*

**Note:** Use fresh marshmallows for best results.

**Microwave Directions:**
Microwave margarine and marshmallows at HIGH 2 minutes in microwave-safe mixing bowl. Stir to combine. Microwave at HIGH 1 minute longer. Stir until smooth. Add cereal. Stir until well coated. Press into pan as directed in Step 3.

# Chocolate Peanut Butter Cups

¾ cup sifted confectioners' sugar
¼ cup KARO® Light or Dark Corn Syrup
¼ teaspoon salt
¼ cup SKIPPY® Creamy or Super Chunk® Peanut Butter
1 package (11½ ounces) milk chocolate chips, melted

**1.** Place 36 (1×¾-inch) foil or paper petit four cups on tray.

**2.** In small bowl with mixer at medium speed, beat sugar, corn syrup and salt until smooth. Stir in peanut butter; if necessary, knead until blended.

**3.** Shape scant teaspoonfuls of peanut butter mixture into 36 balls; place on waxed paper.

**4.** Spoon 1 rounded teaspoonful melted chocolate into each cup. Place peanut butter ball in each cup; gently push down. Chill until firm.      *Makes 36 candies*

# Dish of Dirt

**14 OREO® Chocolate Sandwich Cookies, finely crushed (about 1 cup crumbs), divided**
**1 pint chocolate ice cream**
**¼ cup chocolate-flavored syrup**
**Gummy worms, for garnish**
**Prepared whipped topping, for garnish**

In each of 4 dessert dishes, place 2 tablespoons cookie crumbs. Top each with ½ cup ice cream, remaining 2 tablespoons cookie crumbs and 1 tablespoon syrup. Garnish with gummy worms and whipped topping.

*Makes 4 servings*

*Dish of Dirt*

## Color-Bright Ice Cream Sandwiches

▎▎▎

**¾ cup (1½ sticks) butter or margarine, softened**
**¾ cup creamy peanut butter**
**1¼ cups firmly packed light brown sugar**
**1 large egg**
**1 teaspoon vanilla extract**
**1½ cups all-purpose flour**
**1 teaspoon baking soda**
**¼ teaspoon salt**
**1¾ cups "M&M's"® Chocolate Mini Baking Bits, divided**
**2 quarts ice cream, slightly softened**

Preheat oven to 350°F. In large bowl cream butter, peanut butter and sugar until light and fluffy; beat in egg and vanilla. In medium bowl combine flour, baking soda and salt; blend into creamed mixture. Stir in *1⅓ cups "M&M's"® Chocolate Mini Baking Bits.* Shape dough into 1¼-inch balls. Place about 2 inches apart on *ungreased* cookie sheets. Gently flatten to about ½-inch thickness with fingertips. Place 7 or 8 remaining *"M&M's"® Chocolate Mini Baking Bits* on each cookie; press in lightly. Bake 10 to 12 minutes or until edges are light brown. *Do not overbake.* Cool about 1 minute on cookie sheets; cool completely on wire racks.

Assemble cookies in pairs with about ⅓ cup ice cream; press cookies together lightly. Wrap each sandwich in plastic wrap; freeze until firm.

*Makes about 24 ice cream sandwiches*

## Monkey Bars

▎▎▎

**3 cups miniature marshmallows**
**½ cup honey**
**⅓ cup butter**
**¼ cup peanut butter**
**2 teaspoons vanilla**
**¼ teaspoon salt**
**4 cups crispy rice cereal**
**2 cups uncooked rolled oats**
**½ cup flaked coconut**
**¼ cup peanuts**

Combine marshmallows, honey, butter, peanut butter, vanilla and salt in medium saucepan. Melt marshmallow mixture over low heat, stirring constantly. Combine rice cereal, oats, coconut and peanuts in 13×9×2-inch baking pan. Pour marshmallow mixture over dry ingredients. Mix until thoroughly coated. Press mixture firmly into pan. Cool completely before cutting.

*Makes 2 dozen bars*

*Favorite recipe from* **National Honey Board**

*Color-Bright Ice Cream Sandwiches*

# Peanut Butter Bread

2 cups all-purpose flour
½ cup sugar
2 teaspoons baking powder
½ teaspoon baking soda
½ teaspoon salt
1 cup SKIPPY® Creamy or Super Chunk® Peanut Butter
½ cup KARO® Light or Dark Corn Syrup
2 eggs
1 cup milk

**1.** Preheat oven to 350°F. Grease and flour 9×5×3-inch loaf pan. In medium bowl, combine flour, sugar, baking powder, baking soda and salt.

**2.** In large bowl, with mixer at medium speed, beat peanut butter and corn syrup until smooth. Beat in eggs, 1 at a time. Gradually beat in milk. Stir in flour mixture just until moistened. Pour batter into prepared pan.

**3.** Bake 50 to 55 minutes or until wooden toothpick inserted in center comes out clean. Cool in pan 10 minutes. Remove from pan; cool on wire rack.

*Makes 1 loaf*

# Berry Good Dip

8 ounces fresh or thawed frozen strawberries
4 ounces nonfat cream cheese, softened
¼ cup reduced-fat sour cream
1 tablespoon sugar

**1.** Place strawberries in food processor or blender container; process until smooth.

**2.** Beat cream cheese in small bowl until smooth. Stir in sour cream, strawberry purée and sugar; cover. Refrigerate until ready to serve.

**3.** Spoon dip into small serving bowl. Garnish with orange peel, if desired. Serve with assorted fresh fruit dippers or angel food cake cubes.

*Makes 6 (¼-cup) servings*

*For a super quick fruit spread for toasted mini English muffins or bagels, beat 1 package (8 ounces) softened nonfat cream cheese in small bowl until fluffy. Stir in 3 to 4 tablespoons strawberry spreadable fruit. Season to taste with 1 to 2 teaspoons sugar, if desired.*

## Sweet Treat Tortillas

**4 (7- to 8-inch) flour tortillas**
**4 ounces Neufchâtel cheese, softened**
**¼ cup strawberry or other flavor spreadable fruit or preserves**
**1 medium banana, peeled and chopped**

**1.** Spread each tortilla with 1 ounce cheese and 1 tablespoon spreadable fruit; top with ¼ of banana.

*Sweet Treat Tortillas*

**2.** Roll up tortillas; cut crosswise into thirds.  *Makes 6 servings*

**Cinnamon-Spice Treats:** Omit spreadable fruit and banana. Mix small amounts of sugar, ground cinnamon and nutmeg into cheese; spread evenly onto tortillas. Sprinkle lightly with desired amount of chopped pecans or walnuts. Top with chopped fruit, if desired; roll up. Cut crosswise into thirds.

# Watermelon Slices

**1 package DUNCAN HINES®**
   **Golden Sugar Cookie Mix**
**1 egg**
**¼ cup canola oil**
**1½ tablespoons water**
**12 drops red food coloring**
**5 drops green food coloring**
   **Chocolate sprinkles**

**1.** Combine cookie mix, egg, oil and water in large bowl. Stir until thoroughly blended; reserve ⅓ cup dough.

**2.** For red cookie dough, combine remaining dough with red food coloring. Stir until evenly tinted. On waxed paper, shape dough into 12-inch-long roll with one side flattened. Cover; refrigerate with flat side down until firm.

**3.** For green cookie dough, combine reserved ⅓ cup dough with green food coloring in small bowl. Stir until evenly tinted. Place between 2 layers of waxed paper. Roll dough into 12×4-inch rectangle. Refrigerate 15 minutes. Preheat oven to 375°F.

**4.** To assemble, remove green dough rectangle from refrigerator. Remove top layer of waxed paper. Trim edges along both 12-inch sides. Remove red dough log from refrigerator. Place red dough log, flattened side up, along center of green dough. Mold green dough up to edge of flattened side of red dough. Remove bottom layer of waxed paper. Trim excess green dough, if necessary.

**5.** Cut chilled roll, flat side down, into ¼-inch-thick slices with sharp knife. Place slices 2 inches apart on *ungreased* baking sheets. Sprinkle chocolate sprinkles on red dough for seeds. Bake at 375°F for 7 minutes or until set. Cool 1 minute on baking sheets. Remove to cooling racks. Cool completely. Store between layers of waxed paper in airtight container.

*Makes 3 to 4 dozen cookies*